WHY IS MOMMY HAVING SURGERY?
SHE LOOKS OK TO ME!

FOR FAMILIES WITH BRCA RISK AND UNDERGOING PROPHYLACTIC SURGERY AND RECONSTRUCTION

WRITTEN BY HEATHER BARNARD

ILLUSTRATED BY HANNAH RICHARDSON

Illustrations by Hannah Richardson
Editing by Amy Eisenhard
Layout by Thomas Tran
All rights reserved.

ISBN-13: 978-1514713952
ISBN-10: 1514713950

DURING THIS JOURNEY, I HAD SOME HEROES AND ANGELS I'LL
NEVER BE ABLE TO THANK ENOUGH. WITHOUT THEM, MY FIGHT
WOULDN'T HAVE BEEN SO STRONG.

My husband,
for he is the glue that holds me together, and let's me know it's ok to fall apart.

My children,
for they are my daily inspiration, my reasons for everything I do.

My mother and grandmother,
for teaching me to love life to the fullest. You don't need to worry anymore. XO

Dr. Chrysopoulo,
for he provided unconditional support, took my fears away and humanized my
experience of undergoing a prophylactic mastectomy and reconstruction.

Denise, Courtney and PRMA,
for making me laugh during hard times, for encouragement when I needed it and
for remaining friends beyond my stay.

My friends, my family and my Lovelies,
for they rallied by my side, supporting me every step of the way in their own
individual ways.

FOREWARD

As a reconstructive plastic surgeon specializing in breast cancer surgery, providing high risk patients with their surgical options is relatively straight forward. My job is easy. Not so for you... As with most medical decisions, all options have their pros and cons and the consequences of your decisions, both intended and unintended, can also impact your family.

Thankfully, most patients find support during their decision making process and journey from a spouse, loved one, family or friends. But how do you share your decisions and journey with your young children? How, when and what do you share so they understand what is happening in an appropriate way?

This book is a wonderful tool for starting open and honest conversations with your children. It will help ensure their questions are answered and ease their fears. After all, their experience of your journey may impact their own future healthcare decisions.

MINAS CHRYSOPOULO MD, FACS
PRMA PLASTIC SURGERY
CENTER FOR ADVANCED BREAST RECONSTRUCTION

This story was written using the conversations my family had throughout the process of planning for and having a prophylactic double mastectomy with implant reconstruction. I documented everything in my blog, which allowed me to accurately recount our experiences in this story. Most important was explaining the damaged BRCA gene, which I carry, and why the surgery was so important.

I wrote this candid and honest story to share our journey in hopes of helping you and your children along yours.

"Mommy, why were you telling Daddy you'd be in a hospital?" asked Casey as she came over to sit by her mommy.

Casey's mommy smiled at her and called for her brother and sister, Stewart and Sky, to come sit with them.

With her children by her side and their daddy nearby, their mommy began to tell them her exciting news. "We're going to take a trip this summer, back to the USA, so that Mommy can have a special surgery.

"What kind of surgery Mommy?" curious little nine-year-old Casey asked.

"I've told you before that there's all different types of cancers." She reminded them about brain, skin and lung cancers, and she then explained that women and men can get cancer in their breasts, too. She stopped for a moment, noticing their eyes open wide as they stared back at her with anticipation.

She continued carefully, "Well, Mommy's mommy had cancer and the doctors couldn't help her, no matter what they tried. She had cancer in her breast, called breast cancer. But now, after all this time, doctors are able to help me so that I can be here for you as long as possible."

With her hand raised high waiting her turn to talk, six-year-old Sky anxiously asked, "Mommy, can you catch cancer?"

"No honey, you can't catch it."

"Mommy has wanted this surgery for a very long time" explained Daddy. "We want to make sure you know all about it so that you can ask all the questions you want along the way."

Stewart, the oldest of the children at ten years old, was confused. He didn't understand what his mom and dad were saying. "You have *wanted* this surgery? Why would you *want* a surgery?" he blurted out with a twisted look on his face.

"The doctors couldn't save *my* mommy, but luckily, as I was growing up, doctors were working on a very important blood test. The test could tell them if I was likely to get cancer or not. The test looks at your genes, which are the teeny tiny things, passed on from Moms and Dads to kids that make each person unique; like what color hair you have, how tall you will be and what you sound like. They make you who you are. They are so tiny that we can't see them. Sometimes, the genes don't work right, and mommy happens to have one that doesn't. It's broken. It's called a BRCA gene. That means my body won't fight cancer very well if I ever get it."

"Mommy, do you have cancer now?" Casey asked with little tears forming in her bright blue eyes.

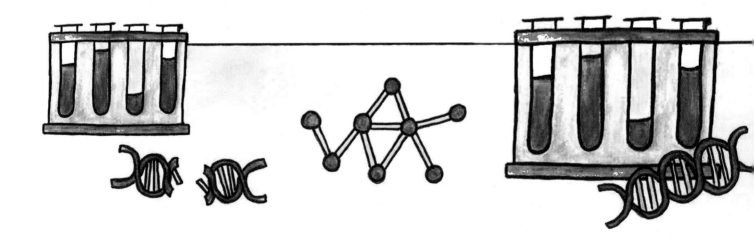

"No, honey, that's where all of this is very exciting for Mommy, because I took the test, the doctors can now try to save me before I get cancer. You know how people can get hips and knees replaced and even get legs and arms made for the ones they don't have? Doctors can do that with breasts too. Mommy is getting hers fixed."

Drawing some images in his mind, while his mom was talking, Stewart was imagining something like robotic arms and metal legs, but couldn't understand how these would fix his mom. So he awkwardly asked, "You mean you're going to have metal ones like the people with metal legs and arms?" The little girls let out little giggles, partly from being embarrassed by the question and partly because they were confused, too.

"No, they won't be metal!" Mommy laughed, "They'll look the same on the outside as they do now, but they are going to take away all my inside tissue that could make me sick, and give me new insides that won't make me sick. They won't be metal; they'll be soft. They'll use a special material. Mommy will still look the same and feel the same when you hug me."

Stewart, Casey, and Sky, along with their Mommy and Daddy, made the long trip from Singapore to Texas, where their mommy would have her surgery. They had many more questions to ask their mommy and daddy the days leading up to the surgery.

Little Sky was finally brave enough to ask the question her brother and sister had also wanted to know. What she really wanted to know was how her Mommy's fixed boobies were going to be made and what they would feel like. So one night while they were all around the dinner table, she mustered up the courage to ask, "Mommy what are your new boobies going to be like?" Happy to help his little girl understand, Daddy explained it in the only way he could to a six-year-old. "Imagine you have a water balloon, but instead of filling with water, it's filled with gummy bears. It's a little squishy and soft."

Sky liked that idea; she imagined her mommy's new boobies full of gummy bears and smiled. "Gummy bears."

Two days later, it was finally time for Stewart, Casey, and Sky to meet their mommy's doctor. They walked into a waiting room and took their seats quietly, watching videos of other families' stories.

Casey turned to her mommy and asked, "Mommy, what will your doctor do to you today? Is today the surgery?"

"Today my doctor is only going to talk to me about my surgery. He'll explain everything that he's going to do during the surgery. He's just going to make extra sure that everything is going to go well so that nobody, even you, will have anything to worry about on the day of surgery."

Casey smiled, feeling assured, and went back to watching the doctors on the TV. She thought it was pretty cool that these doctors could help fix her mommy.

The morning of the surgery finally arrived. Everyone was full of excitement and anticipation.

"Mom, will the surgery hurt?" asked Stewart, concerned for his mom and not wanting her to feel pain.

"Luckily, the doctors are very good at taking all the pain away during the surgery. I won't even know I'm having surgery! They have a special sleepy juice they will give me, and then I'll wake up, like I took a nap. I won't even know I had surgery."

"Can we see you in the hospital when you're done?" asked Sky, hoping to see her mommy as soon as possible.

"Of course you can," her mommy smiled. "Daddy will call you and let you know when the surgery is done so that you know I'm OK. Then grandma will bring you to see me in the morning."

As their daddy grabbed the overnight bag, Mommy kissed her kids goodbye and gave them great big hugs. "Gummy bears," Sky giggled as she hugged her mommy.

"Goodbye! we love you!" The children stood in the doorway with their grandma, all waving and blowing kisses, as they watched mommy get into the car and drive away.

The next morning, the day after surgery, the children were beyond excited to go see their mommy in the hospital. When they saw her eyes starting to open, they said, "Hi Mommy!"

Stewart, Casey and Sky stood at the end of the bed with their grandma. They were unsure of what to do and wanted to be careful. They weren't used to seeing their mommy like this.

"It's ok. You can come closer. You won't hurt me." Their mommy motioned for them to come over and give her a hug.

"Go ahead, give Mommy hugs, it's ok. You won't hurt her." Their daddy prompted them reassuringly.

"Mommy, can we hug you like this?" Sky asked as she gently hugged her mommy from the side, being careful to not hurt her.

"Absolutely, that's the perfect type of hug," as she squeezed her close, then Casey, then Stewart.

After the children had been comforted and put at ease, their mommy began to explain all the new things they were seeing around them. There were funny looking airbags squeezing her legs, which helped her blood flow. There was medicine hanging in a bag and attached to her arm that made her sleepy and talk funny. She even showed them her big, bulky new bra she had to wear to protect her while she healed. The children thought they looked just the same.

The following night, Daddy brought mommy home from the hospital. The children were so excited and so helpful, being very careful around her. As Daddy was helping Mommy get ready for bed, Casey walked into the room as saw her mommy's drains for the first time.

"Mommy, what are those? Do they hurt? " Casey asked, trying not to look, keeping her head turned away. She was uncomfortable.

"These are my drains. They are very important because they are helping Mommy heal. They take away extra fluid my body is making after the surgery. You do not have to look at them if you don't want to. It's OK. I can keep them hidden. Just know that while they are uncomfortable to look at, they are helping me."

Casey eventually got used to the drains and was able to look at them; she even watched her daddy empty them on occasion. Casey knew everything that was happening to her mommy was important, and she wanted to be a part of as much as she could in ahelping her.

After a few days, her mommy didn't need the drains anymore and they took them out at the doctor's office. This made Casey, and her mommy, very happy.

Recovering from the surgery took time, and days passed slowly. Their mommy rested in bed, a lot, for the first week.

She needed help getting dressed because she couldn't raise her arms, help getting in and out of bed because she wasn't strong enough on her own, and help going up and down the stairs so that she wouldn't accidentally slip and fall. She even needed help washing her hair. Mommy needed a lot of help, and the children were very willing to assist.

"Mommy, I'll get that for you," Sky called out as saw her mommy reaching for her bottle of water. Sky quickly grabbed it before her mom could get it, knowing she wasn't supposed to stretch her arms or lift heavy things right away. She held the water as her mommy took some sips and gently placed it back on the side table.

"Mommy, I'll carry that for you!" Stewart hurriedly ran to his mom's side as she tried carrying her computer to her chair. He also remembered hearing that his mommy wasn't supposed to be carrying heavy things, so he took the computer from her as she sat down.

"Mommy, I'll help you put that on," Casey said as she held her mommy's shirt open and low so that her mommy could slip her arms inside.

Another week went by, and mommy was getting better, but still had days that were hard. She got tired easily, she had some aches and pains, and all she wanted was to be able to go out and do fun things with her children.

"Are you OK, mommy? I heard you crying," a concerned Casey entered her mommy's room late one night.

"Mommy's just really tired," explained her daddy. "Mommy is trying so hard to be better for you guys and do more things with you during the day because she loves you so much. It just makes her a little extra tired at night."

Casey climbed up on the bed next to her mom, wrapped her in her blankey and whispered, "I hope you feel better soon." There they sat, together, sharing a special moment in silence.

Three weeks went by, and Mommy was doing really well. She was stronger; she was showering on her own, she was able to carry things, she could get dressed with little help, and she was able to play with her children a bit. One day, she got out of bed, put on a dress and told everyone she wanted to go out and enjoy a special day.

"Mommy, you look pretty today!"

"Mommy, you look like you feel better!"

"I'm really excited you're coming out with us today, Mom."

The children were all so excited to see their mom looking happy. They were happy that she was able to spend time with them.

And most of all, they were excited to know that their mommy had a special surgery so that she could be around for them for a long time.

RIVER WALK

41421947R00020

Made in the USA
Middletown, DE
06 April 2019